LIFE IN AN EGYPTIAN
WORKERS'
VILLAGE

JANE SHUTER

First published in Great Britain by Heinemann Library, Halley Court, Jordan Hill, Oxford OX2 8EJ, part of Harcourt Education. Heinemann is a registered trademark of Harcourt Education Ltd.

© Harcourt Education Ltd 2005
First published in paperback in 2006
The moral right of the proprietor has been asserted.

Produced for Heinemann Library by
    Bender Richardson White
Editors: Lionel Bender, Nancy Dickmann, Tanvi Rai
Designer and Media Conversion: Ben White and
    Ron Kamen
Illustrations: John James, Jonathon Adams and
    Jeff Edwards
Maps: Stefan Chabluk
Picture Researcher: Cathy Stastny and
    Maria Joannou
Production Controller: Kim Richardson and
    Séverine Ribierre

Originated by Ambassador Litho Ltd
Printed in China

ISBN 0 431 113041 (hardback)
09 08 07 06 05
10 9 8 7 6 5 4 3 2 1

ISBN 0 431 113122 (paperback)
10 09 08 07 06
10 9 8 7 6 5 4 3 2 1

British Library Cataloguing in Publication Data
Shuter, Jane
    Life in an Egyptian workers' village. -
(Picture the past)
    932
A full catalogue record for this book is available from the British Library.

Acknowledgements:
The publishers would like to thank the following for permission to reproduce photographs: Ancient Art and Architecture/R. Ashworth p. **28**; Ancient Art and Architecture/R. Sheridan pp. **11**, **25**; Phil Cooke/Magnet Harlequin pp. **6**, **8**, **9**, **12**, **16**, **26**, **27**, **30**; Robert Harding Picture Library/R. Ashworth p. **10**; Trustees of the British Museum, London p. **17** (EA2481); Werner Forman Archive p. **14**; Werner Forman Archive/British Museum, London pp. **19**, **23**; Werner Forman Archive/Dr. E. Strouhal pp. **22**, **24**; Werner Forman Archive/Egyptian Museum, Turin p. **18**; Werner Forman Archive/Louvre Museum, Paris p. **20**; Werner Forman Archive/University College, London, Petrie Museum p. **21**.

Cover photograph of a tomb painting of craftsmen working in a jewellery workshop reproduced with permission of Werner Forman Archive, Bristish Museum, London

Every effort has been made to contact copyright holders of any material reproduced in this book. Any omissions will be rectified in subsequent printings if notice is given to the publishers.

Any words appearing in bold, **like this**, are explained in the Glossary.

www.heinemann.co.uk/library
Visit our website to find out more information about **Heinemann Library** books.

To order:
☎ Phone 44 (0) 1865 888066
📄 Send a fax to 44 (0) 1865 314091
💻 Visit the Heinemann Bookshop at www.heinemann.co.uk/library to browse our catalogue and order online.

ABOUT THIS BOOK

This book is about daily life in the ancient Egyptian village of Deir el-Medina. The village was specially built for the workers who constructed the tombs of some of the **pharaohs**, the rulers of ancient Egypt. The ancient Egyptian civilization lasted from about 3100 BC to 30 BC. The workers needed to live near the tombs in the Valley of the Kings, on the west side of the River Nile. Also, the pharaohs wanted them to live away from other people, to keep the secret of exactly where the tombs were. Ordinary Egyptians lived on the east side the River Nile.

We have illustrated this book with photographs of objects from ancient Egyptian times and artists' ideas of what Deir el-Medina was like. These drawings are based on the remains of the town and its tombs that have been found by **archaeologists**.

The author

Jane Shuter is a professional writer and editor of non-fiction books for children. She graduated from Lancaster University in 1976 with a BA honours degree and then earned a teaching qualification. She taught from 1976 to 1983, changing to editing and writing when her son was born. She lives in Oxford with her husband and son.

Contents

Pyramids and tombs

The ancient Egyptians believed that they came back to life after they died. So they buried people with all the possessions and food they needed for the afterlife. The **pharaohs** began to prepare their burial tombs as soon as they became king. The **pyramids** are the most famous tombs, but pharaohs were also buried in tombs cut into the rock in the Valley of the Kings, near Thebes. Making their tombs was a full-time job for many workers. These workers lived in villages such as Deir el-Medina, built close to the tombs.

Look for these:
The death mask of a pharaoh shows you the subject of each double-page chapter in the book. A scarab bracelet shows you boxes with interesting facts and figures about ancient Egyptian tomb workers' villages.

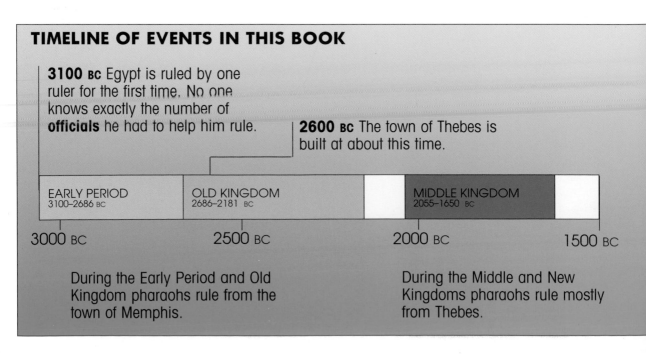

TIMELINE OF EVENTS IN THIS BOOK

3100 BC Egypt is ruled by one ruler for the first time. No one knows exactly the number of **officials** he had to help him rule.

2600 BC The town of Thebes is built at about this time.

| EARLY PERIOD 3100–2686 BC | OLD KINGDOM 2686–2181 BC | | MIDDLE KINGDOM 2055–1650 BC | |

3000 BC   2500 BC   2000 BC   1500 BC

During the Early Period and Old Kingdom pharaohs rule from the town of Memphis.

During the Middle and New Kingdoms pharaohs rule mostly from Thebes.

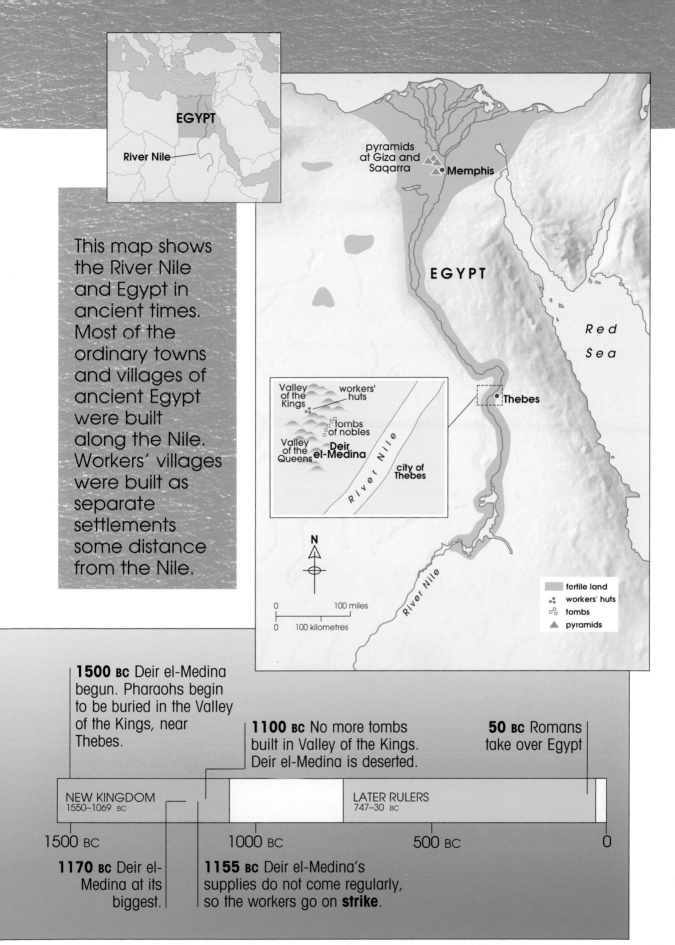

EGYPT

River Nile

pyramids
at Giza and
Saqarra • Memphis

EGYPT

Red
Sea

Valley
of the
Kings

workers'
huts

tombs
of nobles

Valley
of the
Queens

Deir
el-Medina

city of
Thebes

River Nile

• Thebes

River Nile

River Nile

N

0   100 miles
0   100 kilometres

fertile land
workers' huts
tombs
pyramids

This map shows the River Nile and Egypt in ancient times. Most of the ordinary towns and villages of ancient Egypt were built along the Nile. Workers' villages were built as separate settlements some distance from the Nile.

1500 BC Deir el-Medina begun. Pharaohs begin to be buried in the Valley of the Kings, near Thebes.

1100 BC No more tombs built in Valley of the Kings. Deir el-Medina is deserted.

50 BC Romans take over Egypt

| NEW KINGDOM 1550–1069 BC | | LATER RULERS 747–30 BC | |

1500 BC   1000 BC   500 BC   0

1170 BC Deir el-Medina at its biggest.

1155 BC Deir el-Medina's supplies do not come regularly, so the workers go on **strike**.

Deir el-Medina

The workers who built the tombs in the Valley of the Kings lived with their families in Deir el-Medina (sometimes just called Deir). The village was on the other side of a mountain from the tombs themselves. Deir was begun in about 1500 BC. There were 20 houses, opening on to one street, inside a mud-brick wall. Over the next 400 years, the village grew until there were 68 houses inside the wall and another 50 outside it.

Because the villagers had to live close to the Valley of the Kings – seen here – they lived in the desert, where there was no water and they could not grow plants. So the **pharaoh** they worked for had to provide them with everything they needed.

The number of families living in Deir varied, depending on how much work there was to do in the latest royal tomb. There were never fewer than 30 families. The highest number of families was 120. Only the tomb workers and their families lived in Deir. The servants, who did their washing or made their food, all lived by the River Nile.

THE CAMP

All the tomb workers were men. They stayed crammed together for several days at a time in a camp of small huts a few minutes' walk from the tombs. They left their families behind in Deir more than a mile away.

This picture shows ordinary workers' homes and the village outer wall. The chief workmen, who were in charge, lived in the largest houses.

The workers

The most important workers at Deir were the chief workmen. They each ran two groups of workers, one working on the right side and one on the left of a tomb. The groups varied, depending on the work each tomb needed. At first, mostly stone cutters were required, to dig out the passageways and tomb. Later, artists were needed, to draw, carve and paint designs on the walls of the tomb. Other workers included a special police force, to guard all the tombs.

The houses at Deir had stone foundations made from the rock dug from the tombs. Mud-brick walls were built on the foundations. The homes were built for the workers, on the **pharaoh's** orders. These foundations can still be seen today.

As well as making the tombs, workers at Deir made things to go in them. The ancient Egyptians buried their dead with all the things they needed for their next life – clothes, furniture, food, jewellery and even models of servants and boats. Pharaohs and their families were buried with large amounts of very beautiful and valuable possessions.

WAGES

The pharaoh paid the workers mostly in **grain**, which they used to make bread and beer. He also gave them homes, food, water, clothes and pots. He hired servants for the villagers. The servants brought everything up to the village on foot or by donkey. Water and vegetables were brought daily, other things weekly.

The workers of Deir also made tombs in a nearby site, called the Valley of the Queens, for the families of the pharaohs and other important people.

Families

The people of Deir, like all ancient Egyptians, thought families were important. One reason for this was they believed people needed to be cared for even after they died. The best way to do this was to have many children. Men and women were seen as married when they set up home together – there was no marriage ceremony. Women married from the age of fourteen, men from twenty.

This section of a painting from the wall of his tomb shows the chief workman Anherkau and his family. His wife sits next to him. One of their sons can just be seen, standing in front of them, as can two grandchildren playing at their feet.

Many of the workmen at Deir were related to each other. We know this because **archaeologists** have found lists of who lived in the houses. These lists also show that many families had older relatives – often grandparents, uncles and aunts – living with them. Ancient Egyptians were expected to look after relatives who were old, sick, or too poor to look after themselves.

WOMEN

Women at Deir did not work on the tombs. They looked after their families and ran the home. Some women cleaned and cooked for the unmarried men of the village. The men paid them with food from their wages, or with household items such as mats or baskets.

The women of Deir made their own bread. However, the **pharaoh** had special breads and cakes made for the villagers for feast days. These were made in bakeries like the one in this ancient model found in a tomb.

Hard work

It took workers many years to dig out and decorate a tomb. The first job was to dig deep into the rock, to make the burial room. The stone cutters dug out several passages that led nowhere or to empty rooms, as well as to the real tomb. This was to trick anyone who broke into the tomb trying to steal the beautiful things inside. The stone cutters also had to make shafts to the top, so air could move around inside while people worked there. Even so, it was baking hot inside.

The workers dug out the tomb passages and rooms using only hand tools. It was hard, back-breaking work.

NEXT IN LINE

The stone cutters were followed into the tomb by workers who smoothed the walls, floors and ceilings. Next, plasterers moved in and covered the walls and ceilings with a layer of smooth, white plaster. The entrance to the tomb was fully decorated by artists while the stone cutters were still at work, deep inside.

Tombs were carefully planned. There are 24 tombs in the Valley of the Kings. Some are close together. The planners had to make sure the stone cutters did not dig into another tomb. The stone cutters could hear if they were getting too close to a passage as the noise of their digging made an echo. If the echo was too loud, they changed direction sharply.

The stone cutters had only simple stone and **copper** axes to dig with. Slaves that lived in the village, sent there by the **pharaoh**, hauled away the stone in rope baskets.

Once the tomb was dug and plastered, artists moved in to make it beautiful. First, they sketched pictures and **hieroglyphs** in red. Once they were sure everything fitted, they went over the images in black, adding more detail. Sometimes carvers then went around the black lines, to make everything stand out. All tombs were then painted in bright colours. Most colours came from plants or ground-up rocks.

LIGHT

To see in the darkness, tomb workers used lamps that burned animal fat, with salt added to stop the lamps smoking and staining the walls. The workers also reflected light down the passages, using sets of bronze mirrors.

The **pharaoh** Horemheb's tomb was not finished by the time he died. The walls were left as they were, so now we can see the different stages of the artists' work.

Artists had to follow rules. People's faces and bodies had to be shown from the side. Both shoulders had to be shown, even though a person cannot easily stand this way. Men had to have darker skins than women. Black was the colour of death and preservation, so **mummies** were shown as black. Things had to be perfect, so people were shown wearing their best clothes.

Artists painted patterns as well as people, gods and hieroglyphs. However, the most important thing was to show the tomb owner and his family. In this tomb they are on the left-hand pillar.

Houses

Most homes in Deir had three rooms. The first room was small and was often used as a **shrine** to pray to the gods and goddesses. The next room was bigger and taller. It was where the family lived, ate and slept. A smaller room off this one was used for sleeping or storage, depending on how many people there were in the family.

Homes in Deir were built from mud bricks. This modern Egyptian is making mud bricks for houses with the same kind of wooden frame as has been found from ancient Egyptian times.

At the back of the house were steps leading up to the roof. Families spent a lot of time on the roof, where it was cooler than indoors because of the breeze. They often worked, cooked and ate there. On the other side of the stairs was a walled **courtyard**. Here was a bread oven, storage for **grain** and a grinding stone to turn the grain to flour for bread.

This wooden stool was found by **archaeologists** in the tomb of a worker from Deir. The workers mostly had simple wooden furniture. Chairs and tables were often made to fold, or made very lightweight, so they could be carried to and from the roof of the house.

The people of Deir el-Medina walked everywhere. They did not travel far. Families stayed in the village, while the workers usually only made the trip to and from the Valley of the Kings. They carried loads on their backs, in baskets. Food, water, laundry and other things were brought up to the village either by donkey or by servants. Because the villagers were working for the **pharaoh** far from any town, he had to provide everything they needed.

Supplies for Deir were brought across the River Nile from Thebes each day. Donkeys were kept on the west bank of the river, ready to make the journey of 4.8 kilometres (3 miles) to Deir and back. The donkeys in this picture are carrying **grain**.

A BAD DEAL

A villager called Menna gave a man who brought water to Deir a shawl, a headcloth, a pair of sandals, a sack of flour and a sack of grain to take to Thebes and trade them for a donkey. The water carrier tried to cheat Menna by bringing him old or sick donkeys. The chief workmen had to be called in to get Menna a fair deal.

Bread and grain were two of the most swapped items in Deir. Women often made more bread than their families needed, so they had something to swap. This is a model of a servant girl carrying a basket of bread and meat.

The villagers **traded** with each other for things they needed. **Archaeologists** have found records of trade in clothes, food and household items. Most trades worked out fairly because the villagers did not want to cheat each other and cause upsets. For example, the wife of one worker gave another villager a ring, trusting her promise to swap it for a **tunic** in ten days' time.

Education

In ancient Egypt, most children did not go to school but were taught the same skills as their parents. Mothers taught girls to run a home and bring up children. The girls learned to weave and make clothes. Boys were taught by their fathers. In Deir, the children of the stone cutters and slaves began to help clearing the rubble from the tombs from as early as when they were six years old.

The sons of the workmen who made the furniture and other possessions for the tomb began by sweeping up the workshop and fetching and carrying for the older workers.

Reading and writing were skills that only the children of **scribes** were taught. Deir had many scribes. They were needed by the **officials** who ran the village, the storekeepers who looked after the equipment, the artists who decorated the tombs and the people who decorated the possessions for the tombs. There was probably a scribe school in the village.

JOB-HUNTING

In Deir, there was often a shortage of jobs. One father gave two chief workmen and other scribes 'presents' to find his son work. He gave both chief workmen a wooden chair, and one a wooden box, too. He gave one official a folding chair and footstool, the other a leather sack.

Scribes were taught to work sitting down, with their papyrus scrolls stretched out over their knees.

Clothes

Just like all ancient Egyptians, everyone at Deir dressed to keep cool. Many people shaved their heads, too. When the men were working in the hot tombs they probably wore nothing at all, or only a twist of cloth round their waists. The more important workers, such as the chief workmen or the **officials** in charge of the stores, wore longer cloth **tunics**.

Clothes in most ancient Egyptian paintings often look tight-fitting, especially dresses. Real clothes, like this tunic, were looser and easier to move around and work in. Clothes were made from linen, a fabric woven from the stems of flax plants.

Women wore tunics that went down at least to the knees. Young children often wore nothing. Their heads were shaved, except for one place on the side of their head, where the hair was allowed to grow and was plaited. This was called the 'sidelock of youth'. Boys and girls wore it until it was shaved off when they were seen as grown up, sometime between their tenth and thirteenth birthdays.

For parties, people wore complicated wigs over their shaved heads. They often put a piece of scented fat on top of the wig. When the fat melted in the heat, it soaked into the wig and gave off a nice smell.

Free time

The workers at Deir were supposed to work for eight days and then have two days off. However, lists that were found at Deir by **archaeologists** show that workers seldom spent more than three days out of four at work without a day off. Some of these breaks from work were **religious festivals**. Others were days off for special jobs at home, or because of illness.

The chief workmen did not spend their days off doing repairs or making beer. Servants did that for them. They relaxed with their family, played board games or listened to music played by slaves.

The workers at Deir also spent their spare time making their own tombs. These were not as big, beautiful or as full of possessions as the tombs of the **pharaohs**. The workers' tombs were in the cliffside just outside the village. The workers **traded** their skills – a stone cutter dug out the tomb of a carver and of an artist, and they decorated his tomb. The workers also spent time with their families and took part in religious feasts and festivals.

DAYS OFF

Personal reasons for days off included:
- to brew beer
- sickness
- to stay with your wife who was having a baby
- to repair your house.

Senet was a board game, similar to chess, that many ancient Egyptians played. This box would have been expensive, but workers could play the game with a handful of stones and a board scratched out on a rock.

Religion

The workers of Deir and their families, like all ancient Egyptians, believed in many different gods and goddesses, each running a different part of everyday life. The villagers at Deir prayed to the gods and goddesses at **shrines** in their homes and at **chapels** near the village. Several of the workmen were also **priests** at these chapels. Through most of the ancient Egyptian period, priests also did other jobs in villages and towns.

The gods and goddesses of ancient Egypt were often shown with human bodies and the heads of animals. This falcon-headed god is Re, the Sun god.

Once a villager was dead and buried, the family had to visit the chapel above the tomb regularly and leave food and other offerings. In return, the dead person was supposed to speak to the gods and goddesses to get them to help their family.

Religious festivals, such as the festival of the god Min at the start of the harvest, were held in the village regularly. Workmen were given at least one day off. Statues of the gods and goddesses were often carried through the streets, and there was singing and dancing. Animals were killed, offered to the gods and goddesses, then eaten by the villagers. The other regular religious ceremonies were burials in the tombs.

Food

All the food and water for the workers at Deir had to be brought across the River Nile and then up to the village by donkey, 4.8 kilometres (3 miles) from the river. The villagers could store **grain** and dried food, such as beans and fish, but they needed fresh water and vegetables regularly.

FEAST

When workers gave a party, they could not feed everyone. So each guest brought something with them. At one party, 19 people between them brought: 83 loaves of bread, a sack of grain, a cask and a jar of beer, 7 bundles of vegetables and 10 cakes.

These servants are making wine by treading on grapes to press the juice out of them. They are holding on to ropes so as not to fall into the goo.

An Egyptian recipe – Ful

This recipe has been handed down over and over from ancient times. It was a useful dish because it was made with dried beans, which store well. Dried beans have to be soaked overnight, then boiled several times for several hours. It is quicker and easier to use tinned beans. WARNING: Ask an adult to help you with the cooking.

You will need:
1 450 g tin of broad beans
2 eggs
1 lemon
1 clove of garlic, crushed and chopped
salt and pepper
2 sprigs of parsley
a pinch of cumin

1 Put the eggs in a pan of cold water with a tablespoon of salt. Bring to the boil and cook for 8 minutes.

2 Drain off the boiling water and leave the eggs standing in cold water to cool.

3 Open the tin and drain the beans over the sink in a sieve. Rinse them with cold water, then put in a saucepan with a tablespoon of water and the juice of the lemon.

4 Heat the mixture gently, adding salt, pepper, cumin and garlic.

5 Chop the parsley. De-shell the eggs and cut them in slices.

6 Once the mixture is warmed through, pour into a bowl, put the eggs on top and sprinkle with the parsley.

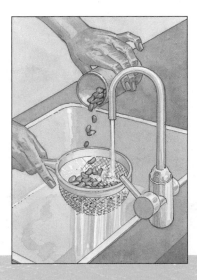

Deir el-Medina now

From 1150 BC onwards, the **pharaohs** paid the workers of Deir less regularly. They even forgot to send food and water. So the workers staged the first recorded **strikes** in history. Some workers even became tomb robbers. From 1108 BC the pharaohs began to lose power, and in 1069 BC there was a time when the country was divided and disorganized. The pharaohs moved to the north of the country, and tried to rule from there, where they built their tombs. The workers moved on, working for **temples** and **officials** near Thebes. Deir was deserted.

Visitors to ancient Egypt can still see the stone foundations of the workers' village of Deir el-Medina. They can also visit some of the tombs in the Valley of the Kings, part of which is seen in this picture.

Glossary

archaeologist person who uncovers old buildings and burial sites to find out about the past

chapel small building for prayer

copper first metal discovered by the ancient Egyptians and used to make sharp edges for swords, spears and farming tools

courtyard open space within, or on one side of, a building

grain fat seeds of several types of grasses known as cereals. Barley, wheat and oats are all grain

hieroglyphs writing of ancient Egypt. The first hieroglyphs were pictures of what people wanted to say. Later, the ancient Egyptians made hieroglyphs that stood for sound, too.

mummy a body preserved by drying and treating with chemicals

official person who helps run a country

pharaoh ruler of ancient Egypt

priest man who works in a temple, serving the gods and goddesses

pyramid large, conical tomb for a pharaoh to be buried in.

religious ceremonies/festivals special times when people go to one place to pray to the god and goddesses

scribe person in ancient Egypt who could read or write. Scribes helped officials and pharoahs to run the country.

shrine place in a house or chapel where people can pray to gods and goddesses and leave them gifts

strike when people stop working for some reason, for example because they are not being paid

temple large building where many people pray together to gods and goddesses and leave them offerings

trade in ancient Egypt, swapping one thing for another

tunic T shirt-shaped clothing that came to at least just above the knee, worn by men, women and children

More books to read

Ancient Egypt: Builders and Craftsmen, Jane Shuter (Heinemann Library, 2000)

People in the Past: Ancient Egyptian Jobs, John Malam (Heinemann Library, 2002)

The Life and World of Tutankhamun, Brian Williams (Heinemann Library, 2002)

Visiting the Past: The Pyramids, Jane Shuter (Heinemann Library, 2002)

Visiting the Past: Valley of the Kings, Ron Alcraft (Heinemann Library, 2000)

Index